Who Was
John F.
Kennedy?

JOHN·FITZGERALD·KENNEDY·

Who Was
John F.
Kennedy?

By Yona Zeldis McDonough
Illustrated by Jill Weber

Grosset & Dunlap • New York

To my children, James and Katherine
McDonough—Y.Z.M.

For Charlotte with love—J.W.

Text copyright © 2005 by Yona Zeldis McDonough. Illustrations copyright © 2005 by Jill Weber. Cover illustration © 2005 by Nancy Harrison. All rights reserved. Published by Grosset & Dunlap, a division of Penguin Young Readers Group, 345 Hudson Street, New York, New York 10014. GROSSET & DUNLAP is a trademark of Penguin Group (USA) Inc. Printed in the U.S.A.

Library of Congress Cataloging-in-Publication Data

McDonough, Yona Zeldis.
  Who was John F. Kennedy? / by Yona Zeldis McDonough ; illustrated by Jill Weber.
    p. cm. — (Who was— ?)
  Includes bibliographical references.
  ISBN 978-0-448-43743-9
  1. Kennedy, John F. (John Fitzgerald), 1917-1963—Juvenile literature. 2. Presidents—United States—Biography—Juvenile literature. I. Weber, Jill. II. Title. III. Series.
  E842.Z9M39 2005
  973.922'092—dc22

2004012225

ISBN 978-0-448-43743-9   20 19 18 17

Contents

Who Was
John F. Kennedy?

The small boat sped quickly along in the dark. It was a hot night in August. The thirteen men onboard were quiet and tense. Their mission was a scary one: They were looking for Japanese warships in the Pacific Ocean.

Suddenly, there was an explosion.

The small boat was ripped in half by a Japanese destroyer returning to its base. Two of the crew were killed instantly. The other eleven men clung to pieces of the boat until morning. Then the wreckage began to sink. The captain decided they all must swim to the safety of a nearby island. The men didn't think they could make it.

"Will we ever get out of this?" asked one.

"It can be done," replied the captain. "We'll do it."

One of the men was burned so badly that he could not swim. He told the captain to save himself and the other men. But the captain would not leave the wounded man. He swam for five long hours with the burned man on his back. When they reached the island, the captain discovered two natives and a canoe.

 He also discovered a coconut shell on which he carved these words:

NATIVE KNOWS POSIT
HE CAN PILOT 11 ALIVE
NEED SMALL BOAT KENNEDY

He gave the shell with the message to the islanders who went by canoe to another island nearly forty miles away. Six days after the patrol boat was destroyed, the brave and quick-thinking captain and his crew were rescued.

The captain's name was John Fitzgerald Kennedy.

Chapter 1
Little Boy, Big Family

On May 29, 1917, a baby boy was born to Joseph P. Kennedy, a wealthy, Irish-American businessman, and his wife Rose. They named him John Fitzgerald Kennedy, in honor of Rose's father—John F. Fitzgerald.

JOSEPH P. KENNEDY

ROSE FITZGERALD

"Honey Fitz" as he was called, had been a popular politician and a former mayor of Boston. When his daughter Rose began dating the young Kennedy boy, Honey Fitz was not so sure he approved. But the couple kept seeing each other and, eventually, Honey Fitz was won over by Joe's hardworking and ambitious nature.

IRISH IMMIGRATION TO THE UNITED STATES

IN THE 1840S AND 1850S, MORE THAN ONE MILLION IRISH IMMIGRANTS SAILED TO AMERICA. BACK IN IRELAND, THE POTATO CROP HAD FAILED. WITHOUT THEIR STAPLE FOOD, AT LEAST ONE MILLION PEOPLE DIED OF STARVATION AND DISEASE. THE IMMIGRANTS WHO CAME HERE WERE CRAMMED INTO CROWDED, DIRTY SHIPS. NEARLY 20 PERCENT OF THEM DIED BEFORE THEY ARRIVED. THE ONES WHO DID WERE CALLED THE "FAMINE IRISH." LIKE MANY NEW IMMIGRANT GROUPS, THEY FACED DISCRIMINATION AND HATRED. THEY COULD NOT EASILY FIND JOBS OR PLACES TO LIVE. SIGNS WITH THE WORDS "IRISH NEED NOT APPLY" WERE COMMON. THEY TOOK THE ONLY WORK THEY COULD GET: LAYING RAILROAD TRACKS, SHOVELING COAL, DIGGING CANALS, AND CLEARING SWAMPS.

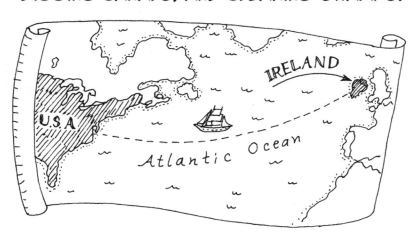

Both the Kennedys and the Fitzgeralds were descended from Irish immigrants. The immigrants had come to Boston, Massachusetts, to escape the terrible potato famine of the 1840s. In the United States, both families had done well.

Nicknamed "Jack," John was the second of Rose and Joseph Kennedy's nine children. They lived in a comfortable clapboard house in Brookline, a town just outside Boston.

THE OTHER KENNEDY KIDS

JOSEPH PATRICK KENNEDY JR. WAS JOSEPH AND ROSE KENNEDY'S FIRST SON, BORN IN 1915. JOHN FITZGERALD, KNOWN AS JACK, WAS BORN IN 1917. ROSEMARY (WHO WAS RETARDED) WAS BORN IN 1918. KATHLEEN, KNOWN AS KICK, WAS BORN IN 1920. EUNICE CAME NEXT, IN 1921. PATRICIA WAS BORN IN 1924. ROBERT, KNOWN AS BOBBY, CAME ALONG IN 1925. JEAN ANN WAS BORN IN 1928. THE NINTH AND LAST KENNEDY BABY, EDWARD, KNOWN AS TEDDY, WAS BORN IN 1932.

TEDDY   JEAN   BOBBY   PAT   EUNICE   KATHLEEN   ROSEMARY   JACK   JOE JR.

When Jack was two-and-a-half years old, he got scarlet fever, a deadly illness. It was so contagious that Jack had to be separated from his mother and baby sister, Kathleen. Jack missed his mother a lot. To take his mind off her, his Irish nanny, Kico Conby, told him wonderful stories about leprechauns and fairies. Usually, Jack loved her stories. But he was so sick, he could hardly listen. Instead, he clutched his favorite teddy bear tightly and drifted in and out of sleep.

Jack didn't get better. His parents rushed him to a hospital in Boston. Strange doctors and nurses came and went all the time. There was no one he knew. He spent weeks in the hospital fighting for every breath. His worried parents hoped and prayed that their little boy would get well again.

Though Jack survived, he was a weak and often sickly child. He suffered from colds, flu, stomach-aches, and allergies, as well as more serious illnesses like bronchitis and diphtheria. To while away the long, boring days spent in bed, he read many books, one after another. His favorite was the story of King Arthur and the knights of the Round Table. Here was a story in which he could get lost: a noble king; his brave men; and their desire to uphold truth, honesty, and justice. Jack's copy grew tattered from so much use.

When he was not sick in bed, Jack tried to be

more like his older brother, Joe Jr. Joe was taller, stronger, smarter, and faster. He could do everything better. How could Jack compete? Jack knew that his father liked winners. There was no tolerance for losers or crybabies in the Kennedy family. To please his father, Jack always played to win, even if it meant putting himself in danger.

Once, his brother Joe dared him to compete in a bicycle race. But this was no ordinary race. They each would ride off in different directions and circle around. When they met up again, the one to swerve first was the loser. Joe was sure Jack would be the first to lose his nerve. But Jack was determined. Faster and faster he pedaled, heading straight for his big brother.

Finally, the two boys were almost face to face. Instead of swerving, Jack recklessly crashed head-on with Joe. He was taken to the hospital, where he had to get twenty-eight stitches. But he refused to lose his nerve in front of Joe. That's how much winning meant to him.

It seemed Jack couldn't please either of his parents. Rose spent a lot of time away from her children. She made trips to Europe to buy the latest fashions. Jack's mother was always scolding him for how sloppy he looked. His shirt was never tucked in; his collar stood up. He was often late for meals, but the family cook took pity on him and fed him in the kitchen.

When Jack was five, Rose planned a three-week trip to California with her sister. Years later, he said, "My mother was never there when we really needed her. My mother never really held me and hugged me."

Jack's father was more fun. In 1929, when Jack was twelve, Joe Kennedy bought a large, white summerhouse with green shutters. It was in Hyannis Port, Massachusetts,

Joe Kennedy's House

John F. Kennedy's House

KENNEDY COMPOUND

on Cape Cod. The house was practically on the beach, facing the Atlantic Ocean. It had a private tennis court and a swimming pool.

Jack's father ran the place like a big summer camp. Every morning, the Kennedy kids had to do exercises out on the lawn. They were drilled by a full-time gym instructor. There were swimming races—even the kids who were six and seven took part. As the children got older, they were taught to sail.

Football games were played on the lawn, and anyone who visited had to join in. In and around Hyannis Port, everyone knew that the Kennedys always played to win.

Thanks to Joe's shrewd head for business, the Kennedy family was rich. And they were growing

richer. Making money was important to Joe Kennedy, and he worked very hard at it. He had graduated from Harvard in 1912 and went into banking. In 1914, at the age of twenty-five, he became one of the youngest bank presidents in the country.

He also began to invest in the stock market. He was good at that, too and built a fortune from his investments. Later on, he began to buy and sell land. He went to Hollywood and dabbled in the

motion picture industry. He met the famous actors and actresses who starred in the films. He also made money from the distribution of liquor. In fact, people said he made money selling liquor illegally. From 1920 to 1933 was the time known as Prohibition. During those years, it was against the law to sell beer, wine, or hard liquor.

Despite the money Joe made, many of Boston's oldest and most respected families still looked down on him. They thought that Joe's

PROHIBITION

IN 1920 THE EIGHTEENTH AMENDMENT TOOK EFFECT—*PROHIBITING* OR MAKING IT ILLEGAL TO MAKE, SELL, OR DRINK WINE, BEER, AND ALCOHOL. SOME PEOPLE FELT DRINKING ALCOHOLIC BEVERAGES WAS IMMORAL. OTHERS FELT THAT PROHIBITION WOULD PUT A STOP TO ALCOHOL'S BAD INFLUENCE ON FAMILY LIFE. BUT WHAT HAPPENED WAS THAT PROHIBITION ENCOURAGED CRIME ON A SCALE NEVER BEFORE SEEN IN AMERICA. SMUGGLING ALCOHOL (BOOTLEGGING) BECAME A BIG BUSINESS. PEOPLE BREWED THEIR OWN ALCOHOL AT HOME. ORGANIZED CRIME, WHICH CONTROLLED MOST OF THE ILLEGAL LIQUOR TRADE, THRIVED. BY 1933 THE GOVERNMENT REPEALED THE EIGHTEENTH AMENDMENT, AND ALCOHOL WAS LEGAL ONCE MORE.

personality was coarse and crude. And they had a strong prejudice against Irish immigrants.

Unlike the old families in Boston, who were Protestants, the Irish were Catholics. Many Irish had been very poor when they first came to America.

Joe worked hard not only to become rich, but also to overcome the negative attitudes people had about him and his family. He wanted his children to have the best and to be the best, too. He would show stuffy, stuck-up Boston just how good the Irish—and the Kennedys—could be.

Yet Joe and Rose wanted their children to understand the value of a dollar. With their allowance, the young Kennedy children were expected to buy birthday and Christmas gifts for the family. When Jack was ten, his allowance was forty cents. At that time, an ice-cream sundae cost ten cents and a comic book, five.

But J‑‑ had become a ‑oy Scout. He needed more money now. So he wrote his father a letter. "When I am a Scout, I have to buy canteens, haversacks, blankets . . . so I put in a plea for a raise of thirty cents for me to buy Scout things and pay my own way more around." Joe was swayed by his son's reasoning. He saved the letter—and gave Jack the raise.

In the fall of 1930, Jack went off to prep school at Canterbury, in Connecticut. But he had a tough time of it. Often lonely and homesick, he came down with a fever of 105 and a terrible case of hives. Over Easter break, the family doctor decided to remove Jack's appendix. He didn't rec... well from the operation. H... never went back to Canterbury.

Instead, the next fall, Jack followed his brother Joe to Choate, a boarding school in Connecticut. Jack was neither an outstanding student nor athlete. He loved reading about history, and he loved to write. He was the only boy at school to subscribe to the *New York Times*. And he was at whiz at trivia questions. There was a popular weekly radio quiz program called *Information Please*. Contestants

had to answer questions on a wide range of subjects. Jack was as good as grown-ups on the program, and his school chums were impressed. Because of his reading, he knew about all kinds of things.

Still, Jack found it hard having Joe as an older brother. When he was grown, Jack said, "Joe was the star of the family. He did everything better than the rest of us." This was frustrating for Jack. He didn't want to be compared to Joe. There was no way he could compete and win.

Instead, it seemed as if Jack tried to be Joe's opposite. Joe was a serious student, so Jack would be casual about schoolwork. If Joe were careful and cautious, Jack would be headstrong and reckless. At boarding school, Jack had helped form the "Muckers' Club." Club members dedicated themselves to playing pranks and practical jokes and just having fun. And Jack liked having fun.

Joe may have been the model child who impressed his parents, as well as his brothers and sisters, with his grades and athletic skills. But Jack was the one who charmed his younger  siblings with his high spirits and zest for life.

The younger Kennedy kids admired Joe. They adored Jack. Jack's favorite sister was Kathleen. They all called her "Kick." Smart, funny, and a little wild, Kick shared Jack's wicked sense of humor. Though there were times Jack felt lost in such a big family, he also loved his sisters and brothers deeply. There was a strong bond among them that lasted all their lives.

Chapter 2
College Life

After Jack graduated from Choate, he decided
not to go to Harvard University. That's where his
father had gone. That's where his brother Joe was
a student. Instead, he chose Princeton University.
Again, Jack wanted to make his own way instead

PRINCETON

of following in Joe's bigger footsteps. Yet Jack wasn't happy at Princeton and soon transferred to Harvard. Although his grades were only average, he still dreamed of glory.

Jack wanted to become a star athlete. He tried out for the football team. During practice, he hurt his back so badly, he had to give up the game.

Instead, he took up swimming. Swimming was fun. And it helped strengthen his back. He joined

HARVARD

the swim team and wouldn't miss practice even when he got sick. One time, he snuck out of the infirmary when he was running a high fever, just to get to practice. He didn't know that his strength as a swimmer would one day help him to save a man's life.

Despite average grades, Jack impressed his college teachers with

his writing and his thinking. Now his family began to see Jack in a new light. Perhaps he might become a reporter or a writer.

At Harvard, his personality made him stand out. Both boys and girls found him charming and funny. He was invited to join one of Harvard's elite clubs. It was a club that had not offered Joe membership. Yet beneath his sunny surface, Jack was often in severe pain. Because he was raised not to complain or cry, he almost never let anyone know how he suffered.

In 1937, while Jack was still at Harvard, his father was made ambassador to Great Britain. The family moved to London. During school breaks, Jack visited. He became fascinated with European politics. He saw the Germans gearing up for war as the other nations anxiously watched.

HITLER AND WORLD WAR II

IN 1933 ADOLF HITLER CAME TO POWER IN GERMANY. HE WAS A MEMBER OF THE NAZI PARTY AND USED VIOLENCE AND FORCE TO ACHIEVE HIS GOALS. HITLER DREAMED OF TAKING OVER THE ENTIRE WORLD. HE STARTED WORLD WAR II BY INVADING POLAND IN 1939. THE POLES OFFERED LITTLE RESISTANCE, AND THIS WAS AN EASY VICTORY. INSPIRED BY HIS SUCCESS, HITLER INVADED DENMARK, NORWAY, FRANCE, BELGIUM, HOLLAND, THE SOVIET UNION, LUXEMBOURG, GREECE, AND YUGOSLAVIA. HE TRIED TO TAKE OVER ENGLAND, BUT THE ENGLISH RESISTED. EVENTUALLY, OTHER COUNTRIES LIKE FRANCE, THE UNITED STATES, CANADA, AND THE SOVIET UNION JOINED FORCES AGAINST HITLER, AND HE WAS DEFEATED IN 1945.

HITLER

Instead of going back to school, Jack took some time off. He spent the spring semester of 1939 in Europe. He traveled to many countries, taking careful notes on what he saw, read, and heard. His travels opened his mind and his heart.

In September 1939, Germany invaded Poland, and World War II began. Jack returned to Harvard, but his time in Europe had changed him. Back at college, he became a serious student. He began to study as he had never studied before. He wrote one very long paper about why England was not prepared for the terrible war. When the paper was finished, he sent it to his father along with a letter that said, ". . . [I]t represents more work than I've ever done in my life."

Joseph Kennedy was very impressed by what he read. He thought Jack's paper was so good that he contacted a publisher. The publishing company agreed with him. In July 1940, Jack's book—*Why England Slept*—became a best seller. A recent college graduate, Jack was now considered an expert on world affairs.

By this time, the war was under way. Italy under Benito Mussolini and Japan under Emperor Hirohito sided with Germany. At first, France and Britain watched and waited. They thought that they might be able to keep peace with Germany rather than fight. But their strategy did not work. France and Britain declared war on Germany.

Then on December 7, 1941, Japan attacked the American military base at Pearl Harbor, Hawaii. Approximately 2,400 people were killed and over 1,100 wounded. The United States declared war on Japan. Japan was Germany's ally. So the United States was fighting Germany as well. For the boys and young men of this country, the long, hard fight had only just begun.

MUSSOLINI

PEARL HARBOR

ALTHOUGH WORLD WAR II HAD BEEN GOING ON IN EUROPE SINCE 1939, AMERICA HAD NOT YET BECOME ACTIVELY INVOLVED. ALL THAT CHANGED ON THE MORNING OF DECEMBER 7, 1941, WHEN THE FIRST WAVE OF 189 JAPANESE BOMBERS MADE A SURPRISE ATTACK ON PEARL HARBOR, AN AMERICAN NAVAL BASE IN HAWAII.

WITHIN TWO HOURS, THE PLANES HAD SUNK OR DESTROYED MANY AMERICAN BATTLESHIPS AND AIRCRAFT. MORE THAN TWO THOUSAND SAILORS AND SOLDIERS WERE KILLED. THE JAPANESE WERE FIGHTING ON THE SIDE OF THE GERMANS. BY DECEMBER 11, 1941, THE UNITED STATES HAD DECLARED WAR ON JAPAN, ITALY, AND GERMANY.

Chapter 3
War Hero

Both Jack and Joe Jr. wanted to fight in World War II. Joe was immediately accepted as a naval air cadet. Jack had to wait. Because of his poor health and old back injury, he failed the physical exam. But Jack was determined to enlist and was eventually accepted into the U.S. navy.

In the spring of 1943, Lieutenant John F. Kennedy was given command of *PT-109*, a patrol boat in the Pacific Ocean. PT stood for patrol torpedo. The boats were light and fast. A PT boat was made of plywood, and only eighty feet long. Many people thought that they were perfect for nighttime missions to stop Japanese destroyers. But others

PT 109

disagreed; the boats were dangerous because they were so small and fragile. Some people felt the boats cost more lives than they saved.

After five months in the Pacific searching for enemy ships, *PT-109* was torn in half by a Japanese destroyer. Once Kennedy realized that the wrecked pieces of the boat would sink, he ordered his men to swim to Plum Pudding Island,

three miles away. Jack refused to leave Patrick McMahon, who was badly burned, to die alone. Instead, he placed Patrick on top of him, back to back. Jack took the long strap from Patrick's life jacket and clenched it in his teeth as he swam. When they finally reached the shore, the end of the strap was scarred with Jack's teeth marks. Jack

had swallowed so much saltwater during the swim that he vomited and then collapsed. Later, aided by the two islanders and the coconut shell he had carved, Jack was able to get help for his men. Other PT boats came to rescue them, and they were able to return to their base on August 8.

Grateful to be alive, Jack was sent home. His

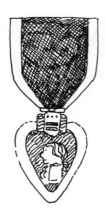

time in the navy had made his old back injury worse. And he had caught malaria. Malaria is a serious disease that causes fever, chills, sweating, and vomiting. He needed to rest and get well again. He was a hero now, and in 1944 received medals from the U.S. navy for his bravery. Yet he remained modest. Later on, a high-school student asked him how he had become a hero. Jack replied, "It was absolutely involuntary. They sank my boat."

Then in August of 1944, not long after Jack's safe return, the Kennedy family's happiness was shattered. Joe Jr. was killed in a plane crash while on a dangerous wartime mission. It was the first of many tragedies to befall the Kennedy family. Though Jack and Joe had been rivals, they were also brothers. They shared a powerful bond, each knowing what it was like to be Joe Kennedy's son. Now Joe Jr. was gone.

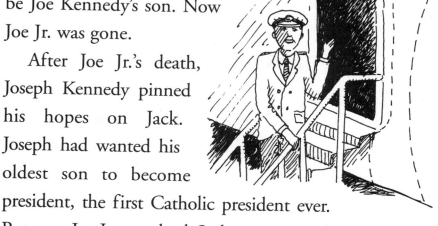

After Joe Jr.'s death, Joseph Kennedy pinned his hopes on Jack. Joseph had wanted his oldest son to become president, the first Catholic president ever. But now Joe Jr. was dead. Jack was next in line.

Jack knew his father wanted him to run for office. He had made that very clear. But did Jack want a life in politics? It would take some soul-searching to find out.

Chapter 4
On the Campaign Trail

Jack had imagined becoming a professor or a writer. Still, his father's pressure, Joe's death, and his own wartime experience changed Jack. Just one year after Joe's death, in 1946, Jack decided to run for Congress from Boston on the Democratic ticket. Or maybe *decided* doesn't quite describe what happened. Here is what Jack said later: "It was like being drafted. My father wanted his eldest son in politics. *Wanted* isn't the right word. He demanded it. You know my father."

Jack hoped to be congressman for Boston's Eleventh District. It was the seat in Congress Honey Fitz, his grandfather, had once held. But first Jack had to beat out ten other candidates who also wanted the Democratic nomination.

When Jack won the primary, Honey Fitz danced a victory jig on a table and sang his trademark song, "Sweet Adeline."

Jack moved into a small apartment at 122 Bowdoin Street in Boston. This remained his voting address for the rest of his life. He now had to get to know the people of Boston's Eleventh District. It was a working-class neighborhood filled with men and women who put in long hours at low-paying jobs.

At first, no one thought Jack could win. He didn't seem like a natural politician. Giving speeches was hard for him. He stuttered and paused. Yet, gradually, he found the words to reach voters.

He spent a lot of time in the navy yards and docks, barbershops and grocery stores, firehouses and police stations. He listened to the stories and complaints of working men and women. Some thought that John F. Kennedy was too rich to represent them. With his private schools and fine houses, how could he understand their needs? To this he replied, "I have an obligation as a rich man's son to help people who are having a hard time of it."

Once, Jack addressed a group of Gold Star Mothers—women who had lost sons in World War II. He talked of the wartime sacrifices people made, the need for peace, and the responsibility of those who survived. He ended by saying, "I think I understand how all you mothers feel. You see, my mother is a Gold Star Mother, too." The women who heard this speech were moved. Afterward, they came up to him, and many told him how much he reminded them of their own sons.

The campaign slogan Jack chose was: "The New Generation Offers Leaders." He promised voters jobs, affordable housing, medical care, and veterans benefits. These promises were not much different from those made by his opponents. But Jack had the Kennedy name and the Kennedy connections. And he was a war hero. In 1944, a well-known writer, John Hersey, had written about Jack and *PT-109* for a magazine called *The New Yorker*. Then Joe Kennedy got the article reprinted in *Reader's Digest*,

which was read by many more people. Now Jack's name was recognized. Later, he regretted using his wartime experiences to help his campaign. "There's something wrong about parlaying a sunken PT boat into a congressional seat."

Jack's big family joined the campaign. His sisters Jean, Eunice, and Pat rang doorbells and handed out leaflets. His mother organized tea parties and receptions. Even Teddy Kennedy, the baby of the family at fourteen, ran errands for his older brother. These efforts—and Jack's own—were rewarded when Jack won the election. In January 1947, Jack Kennedy went off to Washington, D.C., the nation's capital, to serve in the House of Representatives.

CONGRESS

THE UNITED STATES HOUSE OF REPRESENTATIVES AND THE SENATE MAKE UP CONGRESS. (CONGRESS IS THE LAWMAKING BRANCH OF THE FEDERAL GOVERNMENT.) THE MORE PEOPLE THERE ARE IN A STATE, THE MORE REPRESENTATIVES THAT STATE SENDS TO CONGRESS. THE JOB OF THE REPRESENTATIVES IS TO MAKE LAWS. TO DO THIS, THEY ARE BROKEN DOWN INTO COMMITTEES. EACH COMMITTEE DEALS WITH A DIFFERENT ISSUE, LIKE TAXES OR SPENDING.

THE SENATE IS MADE UP OF 100 SENATORS—TWO FROM EACH OF THE 50 STATES. SENATORS USUALLY SERVE ON FOUR OF THE SENATE'S SIXTEEN STANDING COMMITTEES.

A BILL IS ONLY ENACTED (MADE LAW) WHEN IT HAS BEEN PASSED BY BOTH HOUSES OF CONGRESS BEFORE GOING TO THE PRESIDENT. THE PRESIDENT CAN APPROVE OR VETO (REFUSE TO SIGN) THE BILL. IF THAT HAPPENS, THE BILL CAN STILL BE PASSED IF TWO-THIRDS OF BOTH THE HOUSE AND THE SENATE VOTE FOR IT. THAT IS CALLED OVERRIDING A VETO.

Although twenty-nine-year-old Congressman Kennedy looked like a teenager, he had the serious nature of a much older man. He spoke up often and asked many questions. He was not afraid to say what he thought. Jack sponsored a housing bill to help veterans and low-income workers. But the bill was opposed by the powerful American Legion, an organization for former members of the country's armed forces. The legion sided with the real-estate industry, which was against the idea of government helping with housing.

The next year, Jack introduced a bill that would give government money to get rid of slums and provide decent, low-rent housing. Again, the legion fought the bill. This time, Congressman Kennedy spoke out: "The leadership of the American Legion has not had a constructive thought for the benefit of the country since 1918. [The year it was founded.]"

His energy, intelligence, and drive won him two more terms in the House, even though his back continued to cause him great pain. Another blow was the death of his sister Kathleen—Kick—in an airplane crash. He and Kick had been so close, good friends as well as sister and brother. Jack would continue to miss her for the rest of his life.

Jack threw himself into his work. His political dreams grew along with his experience. Though he had entered politics with some reluctance, he wanted to help fix the problems of his country and the world. As the son of Joseph P. Kennedy, he did not have to work. Yet the desire to help others was fired in his soul. "If we're going to change things the way they should be changed, we all have to do things we won't want to do," he said.

After five years as a congressman, Jack was ready for the next step in politics: the Senate. He said, "We were just worms in the House—nobody pays much attention to us nationally." He was frustrated by how slowly things moved in the House of Representatives. It took such a long time for new laws to be made.

In the Senate race, Jack traveled all across his home state to meet the voters. Sometimes, his back hurt so much that he needed crutches.

Henry Cabot Lodge, Jr.

Jack's Republican opponent was the current senator, Henry Cabot Lodge Jr. Lodge came from another important Massachusetts family; his grandfather had also been a politician. In 1944 Lodge had resigned his Senate seat to fight in World War II. He earned the Bronze Star for bravery. Lodge would be hard to beat. Joseph Sr. told Jack, "When you've beaten him, you've beaten the best. Why try for something less?"

Once again, all the Kennedys joined forces to help Jack win the election. Rose gave speeches to churches and civic groups. Along with her daughters, she appeared on a television program shown twice during the campaign called *Coffee with the Kennedys*. Viewers could call in with questions about Jack's childhood. Jack asked his younger brother Robert—everyone called him Bobby—to be his campaign manager. Again, all the hard work and resolve paid off: Jack won the election with 51.5 percent of the vote. The new senator was only thirty-five years old when he was sworn into office.

As senator, Jack represented the interests and needs of the people of Massachusetts. He began to devote himself to issues concerning education, labor, and foreign policy. He hired

twenty-four-year-old Theodore Sorensen as a speechwriter. Sorensen was known for his liberal views, and many biographers feel that he influenced Jack in his way of thinking.

Jack worked so hard that he didn't have time for a wife or family. At a dinner party in 1951, he

was introduced to a lovely young woman. Her name was Jacqueline Lee Bouvier. "Jackie," as she was called, had a refined and sensitive nature. She came from a wealthy family too. "I leaned across the asparagus and asked for a date," Jack said later. Jackie turned him down, but they stayed in touch, even though she went off to Europe.

In 1952, they began dating. Jackie was working as a photographer for the *Washington Times-Herald*. When her newspaper assigned her to England, Jack made an overseas call and asked her to marry him. She said yes.

The couple was married on September 12, 1953, in a Roman Catholic church in Newport, Rhode Island. Seven hundred guests attended the wedding. Another six

hundred came to the party afterward. And
thousands more crowded outside the church

doors, hoping to catch sight of the popular senator
and his pretty bride.

Jackie was a good influence on her new husband. She gave up her own job because she wanted to devote her time and energy to helping him. When he had lived alone, Jack often skipped meals and didn't get enough sleep. But Jackie made sure he ate well, got enough rest, and took care of himself. She also inspired him with her love of art, literature, and culture. After he fell seriously ill and needed a back operation, she was there to nurse him back to health.

While recovering, Jack had time to think about the difficult decisions politicians often make. He began to write notes about how leaders can be torn between doing the right thing and keeping their jobs. His notes grew into a book. It was called *Profiles in Courage*. The book had eight short biographies of senators who had shown

unusual courage by supporting unpopular causes. Leaders like Daniel Webster, John Quincy Adams, Sam Houston, and Robert A. Taft. They had risked their careers in order to remain true to their own beliefs. They were inspiring to Jack. In 1957, Jack's book won the Pulitzer Prize for biography.

Writing the book made Jack think more about his own idealism and goals. He decided to seek the highest elected office in the country. Jack's great-grandfathers had come to America penniless. Now John F. Kennedy wanted to become president of the United States.

Chapter 5
Mr. President

Once he was fully recovered, Jack started campaigning in earnest. He was now forty-two years old. Many people thought he wasn't old enough to be the president. The president who was then in office, Dwight D. Eisenhower, had been sixty-two when first elected. In comparison, Jack seemed so young. Eisenhower referred to Jack as "that boy." People were used to an older man as the leader of the country.

In addition, Jack was Roman Catholic. The country had never elected a Catholic president. The Pope is the head of the Catholic Church. He gives guidance to Catholics on many issues. Some

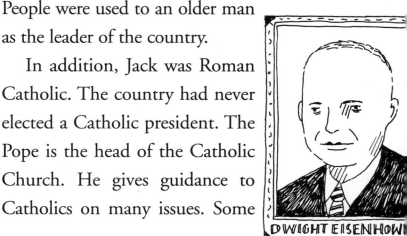

DWIGHT EISENHOWI

people in the United States worried that a Catholic president might be influenced by the Pope. Jack urged people to put aside their worries. His religion was personal. It would not interfere with being president. In speaking to a group of Protestant leaders, he said, "I believe in an America where the separation of church and state is absolute . . .

I am the Democratic Party's candidate for president, who happens also to be a Catholic. I do

not speak for my church on public matters—and the church does not speak for me."

At the 1960 Democratic convention in Los Angeles, California, another man also wanted to run for president. Lyndon Johnson was a powerful senator from Texas. He'd been in Congress for twenty-three years. He was the Senate Majority Leader. He argued that John Kennedy was young and inexperienced.

Yet despite his youth, Jack won the nomination. And the man he wanted to run with him on the ticket was Lyndon Johnson.

Johnson thought about it. Being vice president would give him lots of national attention. It also put him next in line for the presidency, if anything were to happen to Jack. In the end, Johnson agreed to run.

John Kennedy made a speech on TV to accept the Democratic nomination. He stated the themes of his campaign: "We stand today on the edge of a New Frontier . . . Beyond that frontier are uncharted areas of science and space, unsolved problems of peace and war, unconquered pockets of ignorance and prejudice, unanswered questions of poverty and surplus." He wanted Americans to be the "pioneers on that New Frontier." It was a brilliant speech. By stressing the bright promise of the future while reaching back to the pioneer past, Jack tapped the unspoken dreams and hopes of all Americans.

John Kennedy ran against Republican Richard Nixon. Nixon had been vice president under Dwight D. Eisenhower. He told voters that the experience he gained in those years made him a better candidate. He wanted the government to help private businesses. In contrast, Jack Kennedy believed that the government should help make peoples' lives better.

Jack Kennedy and Richard Nixon had a debate, and for the first time in history, the debate was broadcast on TV all across the country. Before the 1950s, most people had only radios in their homes. Now millions of Americans could see the two candidates discussing issues. Under the harsh lights,

Richard Nixon seemed nervous and uncomfortable. In contrast, Jack Kennedy seemed relaxed,

NEW YORK   LOS ANGELES

handsome, and polished. After the debates were over, most people thought Jack was more impressive. In fact, in a poll of four million people who watched the debates, three million voted for Kennedy.

The race was one of the closest in history. On November 8, Election Day, Jack and Jackie Kennedy went to the voting booths in Boston and cast their votes. Then they went to Hyannis Port, where the family still had their big, white summerhouse, to wait for the

results. All the Kennedys stayed up late into the night, but it was still unclear who would win. Finally, everyone went to sleep. At about 2 a.m. on November 9, the answer came.

John F. Kennedy was going to be president of the United States. He was the youngest man—forty-three—ever elected. And the first Catholic.

Jack was disappointed by the narrow victory. He won only 49.7 percent of the vote, compared to Richard Nixon's 49.6 percent. Now, Jack was even more determined to prove himself a great leader.

INAUGURATION

The January day on which John F. Kennedy took the oath of office was bitterly cold. Yet he appeared without a hat or topcoat. He wanted to project an image of strength and youth. By his side was Jackie, who had just given birth to their second child and first son, John Fitzgerald Kennedy Jr. The Kennedy clan, including Jack's father, was there, too. Even though Joseph Kennedy had stayed behind the

scenes—he held many unpopular views and did not want to drive away voters—he was filled with pride at his son's accomplishment.

President Kennedy's speech became famous for these words: "And so, my fellow Americans, ask not what your country can do for you; ask what you can do for your country."

When the Kennedys moved into the White House, America welcomed them with open arms. The new president surrounded himself with "the best and the brightest" people as advisors. His wife was smart, charming, and beautiful—a patron of the arts.

For the first time since the presidency of Theodore Roosevelt sixty years earlier, young children lived in the White House. Caroline Kennedy was three, and her baby brother, John-John, was less than a year old. Jackie didn't like the children to talk to reporters or be photographed. She wanted them to have as normal a childhood as possible. But Jack liked it when

the children were caught on camera. The president would get down on all fours with John-John in the Oval Office. Caroline also loved spending time there. They both would hide under their father's desk and take candy from the dish on the secretary's desk. Caroline once walked in during a press conference wearing her mother's high heels.

The Kennedys brought animals into the White House. They had rabbits, guinea pigs, and two hamsters who escaped from their cages. Jack's favorite pet was a dog named Charlie. Caroline even had a pet pony named Macaroni. She rode him across the White House lawn while her father watched.

Kennedy was a great storyteller. He told tales in which Caroline won horse races and John-John sank a Japanese destroyer in his PT boat. Kennedy also created a character called the White Whale, who liked to eat dirty sweat socks.

Jackie brought her own unique style and vision to the White House. As first lady, she redid the White House with beautiful early American furniture and paintings. She wanted the house to reflect

the country's history and be a place that was equal to the important men and women who came to visit.

Together, the Kennedys hosted dinners to which they invited people from all walks of life. The parties were exciting and glamorous. Jacqueline Kennedy turned the White House into a place of culture and Art with a capital A. Cellist Pablo Casals was a guest, as well as aviator Charles Lindbergh, composer Leonard Bernstein, and songwriter Irving Berlin. Another dinner brought together American winners of the Nobel Prize. Throughout the time he was president, JFK supported the arts. Because of his efforts, the National Endowment of the Arts was created, giving money to encourage artists of all kinds—actors, dancers, musicians, and architects.

Jackie was equally comfortable, whether hosting a poetry reading, a formal dinner, a ballet performance, or a party onboard the presidential yacht.

When the Kennedys went to France, the first lady made a huge hit with President Charles de Gaulle and all the French people. Jack joked that he would be remembered as "the man who accompanied Jacqueline Kennedy to Paris."

Jack loved being president. On a typical day, he was up by seven-thirty. He quickly read several newspapers, had a hot bath, ate breakfast, and dressed. By eight-thirty or nine, he was at work in the Oval Office.

In the basement of the White House, Jackie found a very old desk and had it moved to the Oval Office. It had belonged to President Rutherford B. Hayes. The desk was made of wood from a ship that had been shipwrecked in 1854. President Kennedy loved the desk. The coconut shell with the carved message for help sat on top of it—a reminder of when the *PT-109* had been shipwrecked.

Models of America's greatest sailing ships were also placed around the Oval Office. Kennedy joked about his job: "The pay is good and I can walk to work." With his usual modesty, he didn't add that he gave all his salary to charity.

Kennedy took care of lots of business by telephone. In 1961, politics was still a "face to face"

business. But JFK liked the phone, because it gave him information quickly.

Around noon each day, he swam in the White House pool and did exercises for his back. Then he ate lunch—a hamburger most days, served on a tray. After that, he took a nap and spent an hour with Jackie. By the end of the afternoon, he was back in the Oval Office with the door open, so his staff could come in and ask questions. Often, he saw as many as seventy people in a single day.

Most evenings, he brought work home with him. There were lots of papers to read and to sign. Other nights, he might attend a formal state dinner.

Sometimes, the Kennedys had a small dinner party for friends. Afterward, they watched a movie in the White House theater. On weekends, the first family flew to Hyannis Port. Jack loved to sail and play golf there. In the winter, the Kennedys visited Palm Beach, where Joe Sr. and Rose had a house. It was a busy life, but a productive and happy one, too.

Over the years, Jack tried many ways to ease his back pain. One doctor suggested a rocking chair. The gentle motion might help. So Jack bought a simple thirty-dollar model made in North Carolina. He found it so relaxing that he ordered several more—to have one wherever he was. The image of the young president in a rocking chair became familiar to the American people.

JFK never showed the public how bad the pain was. When he needed crutches, he put them away, out of sight before a speech or public appearance. And he was a big supporter of sports and physical activity for Americans. He expanded the President's Council on Fitness. It encouraged all Americans, old and young, to lead healthy, active lives.

As president, John Kennedy eagerly supported American space exploration. He promised that by the end of the 1960s, an American would land on the moon. He was right. In 1962, John Glenn became the first American to orbit the Earth. It took him four hours and fifty-five minutes to circle the planet three times.

SPACE EXPLORATION: USA VS. USSR

SHORTLY AFTER THE END OF WORLD WAR II IN 1945, U.S. GOVERNMENT SCIENTISTS BEGAN WORKING ON SPACECRAFTS. THESE PILOTLESS, ROCKET-POWERED VESSELS WERE SENT HIGHER AND HIGHER INTO SPACE. BY 1955 SCIENTISTS FELT IT WAS ONLY A MATTER OF TIME BEFORE THEY WOULD BE ABLE TO SEND A SMALL SHIP FILLED WITH INSTRUMENTS INTO ORBIT AROUND THE EARTH. BUT IN 1957 THE UNITED STATES WAS RUDELY SURPRISED TO FIND OUT THAT A SATELLITE CALLED SPUTNIK WAS ALREADY ORBITING THE EARTH. IT HAD BEEN SENT UP BY AMERICA'S RIVAL, THE SOVIET UNION. NOW THE UNITED STATES HAD TO CATCH UP. KENNEDY HAD CONGRESS POUR MONEY INTO THE NEWLY CREATED SPACE PROGRAM CALLED NASA (NATIONAL AERONAUTICS AND SPACE ADMINISTRATION). ALTHOUGH KENNEDY DID NOT LIVE TO SEE HIS DREAM REALIZED, AMERICANS FIRST SET FOOT ON THE MOON IN 1969. THIS TRIUMPH WAS POSSIBLE BECAUSE OF KENNEDY'S SUPPORT YEARS BEFORE.

Kennedy believed that the United States, the richest nation in the world, had to help other, poorer nations. With this in mind, the president set up Food for Peace. Cargo ships filled with food were sent to countries in Africa, Asia, and Latin America, where people did not have enough to eat.

JFK also created the Peace Corps. Young men and women volunteered to spend two years in a needy country where they helped build schools, water wells, health centers, and other projects. Peace Corps volunteers also taught villagers better ways of farming their land.

Right away, more than 5,000 applicants took the exam to be in the Peace Corps. By the end of

1963, 7,500 volunteers were at work in over forty-four countries. By 2002, more than 165,000 Americans had served in the Peace Corps.

Jack picked his sister Eunice's husband to head the Peace Corps. He also brought other family members into his administration. He asked his younger brother, Bobby, to be attorney general. Bobby had run Jack's campaign for president. Now, as attorney general, he would be the head of the Department of Justice and a member of the

ROBERT and JOHN

president's cabinet. His job would be to prosecute in federal cases.

Robert Kennedy was only thirty-six at the time. Although JFK was criticized for this, he wanted someone in his cabinet whom he could trust completely. Bobby was that person.

Lyndon Johnson, the vice president, did not get along with Bobby Kennedy. He often felt left out of important decisions.

In 1962 the youngest Kennedy, Teddy, ran for senator in Massachusetts. He won. It was the same job that his brother Jack had once held. Teddy was only thirty.

Now people saw the Kennedys as a dynasty—the most important family in the United States. Americans had strong feelings about the Kennedys. People either loved them . . . or hated them.

Chapter 6
Facing the Challenges

John F. Kennedy was president for only three years. He made mistakes, but he tried to learn from them, too.

After he took office, there was a plan to overthrow Fidel Castro. Castro was the leader of the Communist government in Cuba. Following World War II, the United States and the Soviet Union were the two superpowers. The United States was a democracy. The Soviet Union was a Communist nation. Each was armed with atomic weapons. Although there was never actual fighting, the tensions between the two nations came to be known as the Cold War.

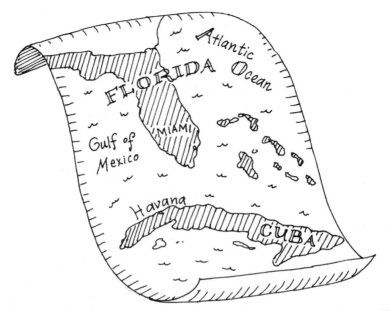

The island of Cuba was only ninety miles off the coast of Florida. Fidel Castro was a powerful ruler. A Communist country so close to the United States was seen as a threat to the United States' safety.

President Kennedy okayed the plan to invade Cuba. An army of exiled Cubans landed at Cuba's Bay of Pigs. The invasion was a complete failure. More than one thousand men were captured and imprisoned in Cuba. Others were killed. When he learned what had happened, John Kennedy spent the whole night awake and pacing the floor. As president, he took full responsibility for the disaster. "All my life I've known better than to depend on the experts," he said. "How could I have been so stupid to let them go ahead?" The Bay of Pigs fiasco made America look bad in the eyes of the world. Other nations accused the president of being badly informed and impulsive.

The greatest crisis of Jack Kennedy's presidency began on the morning of October 16, 1962. Again, it involved the island of Cuba. The president was eating breakfast when an aide interrupted his meal. The Soviet Union had put missiles in

U.S.S.R.

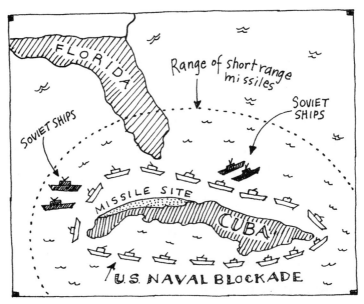

Cuba. The missiles could strike the United States.

Some advisors wanted the president to bomb the missile sites. But then war would break out between the United States and the Soviet Union. The missiles *had* to be removed. They posed too great a danger to the country. What was JFK going to do?

John Kennedy had not forgotten the Bay of Pigs disaster. He knew he had to think—and act— with great care. If he didn't, a war with nuclear bombs could start . . . a war that could destroy the world.

JFK decided to blockade Cuba. He gave orders for one hundred and eighty American ships to sail into the Caribbean. The ships formed a line five hundred miles long. No ships coming from the Soviet Union could get through to Cuba—not unless they attacked the American ships.

When the Russian boats appeared on the horizon, President Kennedy and the rest of the country held their breath. What would happen? Would the Russians attack the U.S. boats, setting off war?

To everyone's relief, the Russian ships turned around and moved away from Cuba. President Kennedy spent the next few days talking with the leader of the Soviet Union, Nikita Khrushchev. Khrushchev agreed to remove the missiles. The

KITA KHRUSHCHEV

two leaders also agreed to limit testing of nuclear weapons.

Like the men praised in his book *Profiles in Courage*, John F. Kennedy remained firm and strong in a time of crisis. His resolve avoided war.

Another issue facing the president and the country was civil rights. Slavery had ended in 1865, almost one hundred years earlier. Yet still black people, especially in the South, did not have the same rights as white people.

In many places, blacks could not mix with whites. They had to live in separate neighborhoods, go to all-black schools and churches. Restaurants, stores, hotels, beauty parlors—even water fountains—had signs "for whites only." On public buses, blacks were forced to sit in the back. A black person had to give up a seat to a white person if there were no other empty seats.

But in the 1950s, blacks began to protest. They insisted on equal rights as citizens. In 1962, an

African-American student, James Meredith, tried to register for classes at the all-white University of Mississippi. The governor, Ross Barnett, denied him the right to attend the all-white school. Many white people gathered at the university. They jeered at Meredith and called him names. They told him to turn around and go home. But Meredith insisted on his constitutional right to enroll. And the next day, President Kennedy called in National Guard troops to stop a riot and to protect James Meredith.

During his presidency, Jack grew ever more

deeply committed to the cause of civil rights. In June of 1963, he told the American people, "One hundred years of delay have passed since President Lincoln freed the slaves, yet . . . their grandsons are not fully free. They are not yet freed from the bonds of injustice, they are not yet freed from social and economic oppression. And this nation . . . will not be fully free until all its citizens are free."

Within days of making this speech, Jack started planning for a new civil rights bill. The bill would protect the rights of African Americans. No longer would hotels, restaurants, movie theaters, and stores be able to turn away black customers. The new Civil Rights Act became law in 1964—less than eight months after John F. Kennedy's death.

Chapter 7
A Sudden End

The next election for president was going to be in 1964. JFK wanted a second term. By late 1963, he was already thinking about his campaign. He decided to travel to Texas, the home state of Vice President Lyndon Johnson. Jack planned to make speeches to a group of businessmen at the Trade Mart in Dallas. He knew that many Texans had voted for Richard Nixon in the 1960 election. And that they were angry over his stand on civil rights. The trip to Texas, with Jackie by his side, would be a good way to "mend fences" with these voters and gain their support.

Many people close to JFK worried about the trip. The crowds in Texas might be unfriendly. But that was not so. At lunchtime, the president's plane touched down at the Dallas airport. A large and cheering crowd came to greet JFK and Jackie, elegant and glamorous in her pink suit and matching pillbox hat. Kennedy commented, "This doesn't look like an anti-Kennedy crowd."

A long procession of cars, called a motorcade, headed through the city. The president and his wife sat at the back of a limousine with the governor of Texas and his wife. Vice President Johnson and his wife were in another car.

The president's limousine had a plastic shield to put over the passengers to protect them from rain.

It could also deflect bullets. But Jack wanted to leave the plastic top off. It was a beautiful day. He wanted to see the crowd. And he wanted the crowd to see him.

As the Kennedys rode through the streets of Dallas, they smiled and waved. One little girl had a sign that said: "Mr. President, will you please stop and shake hands with me?" Kennedy stopped the motorcade to shake hands with the girl.

When the motorcade turned onto Main Street, the crowd was even larger. About two hundred thousand people had gathered to see the Kennedys pass by. The wife of the Texas governor, Nellie Connally, looked at the packed streets and said, "You sure can't say that Dallas doesn't love you, Mr. President."

A moment later, shots rang out.

Someone in the limousine shouted out, "Oh no, no, no!"

The president had been hit.

Jack slumped over toward Jackie. Her pink suit was splattered with blood. The car sped through the streets to the nearest hospital. But it was too late.

Doctors confirmed the awful news: John Fitzgerald Kennedy was dead.

On a plane back to Washington, D.C., Vice President Lyndon Baines Johnson was sworn in as the new president. Jackie Kennedy stood by his side as he took the oath of office.

It is now more than forty years since JFK was killed that terrible day in Dallas. Yet everyone alive at the time remembers where they were when they heard the awful news.

Barely an hour-and-a-half later, a man named Lee Harvey Oswald was arrested for the shooting. Then only two days later, another man named Jack Ruby shot and killed Oswald, right in the Dallas police station— and live on television news!

For more than a year, evidence was gathered on the assassination. Many people did not believe that Oswald had acted alone. People in the crowd said they heard shots coming from two directions. But the official report said that Oswald and only Oswald was responsible for the president's death.

It was as if the whole world, not just the United

States, went into shock. How could something so senseless happen? And to such a young, vital president? JFK's smiling face was on the front page of newspapers on every continent.

On the following Monday, the president's funeral was held in Washington, D.C. World leaders came, kings and queens. The flag-draped coffin was pulled through the streets by a team of white horses. There was also a black horse with no rider. A pair of boots was placed backward in the stirrups. The symbol of a fallen leader.

Dressed in a black suit and veil, Jackie Kennedy stood with Caroline and John-John. As the coffin passed them, John-John raised his hand in a final salute to his father. The image of the little boy saying good-bye was captured in one of the most famous photographs of all time.

The horses kept moving slowly. Soon, they reached Arlington National Cemetery in Virginia. There, John Fitzgerald Kennedy was laid to rest. An eternal flame was lit beside his grave.

Like the legendary King Arthur, whom he had admired as a boy, John F. Kennedy tried to be a fair, brave, and honorable leader. He inspired a nation to hope and dream for a better future. He was president for only one thousand days. Yet John F. Kennedy still holds a special place in the hearts of all Americans.

JOHN·FITZGERALD·KENNEDY·

Timeline of John F. Kennedy's Life

1917	Born to Rose and Joseph Kennedy in Brookline, Massachusetts
1940	Graduates from Harvard College
1940	Publication of *Why England Slept*
1941	Enlists in the U.S. navy
1943	*PT-109* destroyed; Kennedy rescues the remaining crewmen
1944	Joseph P. Kennedy Jr. dies while on a secret wartime mission
1946	Elected to the U.S. House of Representatives
1952	Elected to the U.S. Senate
1953	Marries Jacqueline Bouvier
1957	Daughter Caroline is born; awarded Pulitzer Prize for *Profiles in Courage*
1960	Wins Democratic presidential nomination; gives "New Frontier" speech
1960	Elected thirty-fifth president of the U.S.; son John Fitzgerald Kennedy Jr. is born
1961	Establishes Peace Corps
1961	Meets with Soviet Premier Nikita Khrushchev
1961	Bay of Pigs invasion fails
1962	Cuban Missile Crisis
1963	Submits civil rights bill to Congress
1963	Assassinated in Dallas, Texas

TIMELINE OF THE WORLD

World War I begins in Europe	1914
The United States enters World War I	1917
U.S. ratifies the Nineteenth Amendment to the Constitution, giving women the right to vote	1920
The word "robot" enters the language via Karel Capek's play *R.U.R.*	1921
Kodak introduces home movie equipment	1923
Little Orphan Annie enters the comics pages	1924
Three million radio sets in the U.S.	1924
Disney adds sound to cartoons	1928
Great Depression begins in the U.S.	1929
Pluto discovered	1930
Empire State building completed	1931
Amelia Earhart becomes the first woman to fly solo over the Atlantic Ocean	1932
Franklin Delano Roosevelt elected president of the U.S.	1932
Adolf Hitler becomes chancellor of Germany	1933
Cheeseburger invented	1934
World War II begins in Europe	1939
Modern helicopter invented	1939
Pearl Harbor bombed by Japan; America enters WWII	1941
A Tree Grows in Brooklyn by Betty Smith published	1943
Smokey the Bear starts fighting forest fires	1944
World War II ends	1945
The Diary of a Young Girl by Anne Frank published	1947
Disney's animated classic *Peter Pan* released	1953

1955 —— Rosa Parks, a black woman, refuses to give up her seat on a bus in Montgomery, Alabama; modern civil rights movement is born

1957 —— Sputnik sent into orbit by Soviet Union

1958 —— An Elvis Presley concert in Chicago sends twelve thousand fans into screaming hysteria

1959 —— Barbie doll introduced

1960 —— Domino's delivers its first pizza

1961 —— Harper Lee wins Pulitzer Prize for *To Kill a Mockingbird*

1962 —— *Dr. No* begins James Bond series

1963 —— Martin Luther King Jr. delivers "I Have a Dream" speech

BIBLIOGRAPHY

Cooper, Ilene. **Jack: The Early Years**. Dutton, New York, 2003.

Leaming, Barbara. **Mrs. Kennedy**. Touchstone, New York, 2001.

Milton, Joyce. **John F. Kennedy**. DK Publishing, New York, 2003.

Randall, Marta. **John F. Kennedy**. Chelsea House Publishers, New York, 1988.

Silver, Kenneth E. **JFK and Art**. Bruce Museum of Arts and Sciences, Greenwich, Connecticut, 2003.

Spies, Karen Bornemann. **John F. Kennedy**. Enslow Publishers Inc., Berkeley Heights, NJ, 1999.

Uschan, Michael V. **The Importance of John F. Kennedy**. Lucent Books, San Diego, CA, 1999.